Obtaining Restoration in the Courts of Heaven: Courtroom Prayers for All Round Restoration

The author is aware that the application of this book may differ from one person to another as such things as faith, persistence, trust, and love for God can determine the outcomes that you receive from the application of the principles in this book.

TABLE OF CONTENTS

YOU URGENTLY NEED THIS

I don't know what you've lost, but something is telling me to tell you that God led you to the contents of this book for the right reasons, so that you can have everything that you have lost restored.

Why do you sit down every day regretting and mourning over that which you have lost? What is the essence of the tears? Can you restore a single thing even if you decided to cry from now till tomorrow? I am sure that you can't restore nothing.

But I will show you what to do. I don't know what you have lost, but whatever it is, it can be restored back to you in the courts of heaven. I will only say this, if you don't want to be surprised by the type of restoration that you are going to be experiencing, then this book might not be for you. May be I am talking to the wrong person. But I know that I am not because since you are reading the pages of this book, I know that you are the right person and after concluding what has been outlined in the pages of this book, you will have what you've lost.

CHAPTER 1

The Basis of Restoration

Never listen to anything that I am about to say to you if what you are about to read has no scriptural basis. The reason why we are teaching these things today is because the scripture has said it, and we are confident that when the bible has said it, then we are sure that what we are teaching manifestations can follow it.

Joel 2:25

> *And I will restore to you the years that the locust hath eaten, the cankerworm, and the caterpiller, and the palmerworm, my great army which I sent among you.*

In the scripture under reference, we see God talking to his people that he will make a restoration of all that the devil has taken from you. One thing caught my attention that he will not only restore to you the things that the enemy has taken from you, but he will also restore to you the time that the enemy has stolen from you. Now let me explain this to you. God was speaking to the people that I will restore to you all that the enemy has stolen from you. Imagine a man who was rich through the blessings of the Lord, and the devil came and attacked all the resources that he had. This was a man who was living in abundance, but the devil came and took away that which he has. He was back to level zero. God said I will not only restore to you the financial resources which the devil has taken from you, but I will restore to you the time that the devil has taken. If it would have taken that man another ten years to make 5 Billion dollars, God says, I will restore to you the lost years by giving you that money now.

Friends, that is the basis of our bold statement when we said that the Lord will restore to you all that the enemy has taken from you. So what we are dealing with is an assurance to us that the Lord will do a restoration in our lives.

CHAPTER 2

Walking with the God of Restoration

The Ass

1 Samuel 9:1-20

> *Now there was a man of Benjamin, whose name was Kish, the son of Abiel, the son of Zeror, the son of Bechorath, the son of Aphiah, a Benjamite, a mighty man of power.*
>
> *2 And he had a son, whose name was Saul, a choice young man, and a goodly: and there was not among the children of Israel a goodlier person than he: from his shoulders and upward he was higher than any of the people.*

3 And the asses of Kish Saul's father were lost. And Kish said to Saul his son, Take now one of the servants with thee, and arise, go seek the asses.

4 And he passed through mount Ephraim, and passed through the land of Shalisha, but they found them not: then they passed through the land of Shalim, and there they were not: and he passed through the land of the Benjamites, but they found them not.

5 And when they were come to the land of Zuph, Saul said to his servant that was with him, Come, and let us return; lest my father leave caring for the asses, and take thought for us.

6 And he said unto him, Behold now, there is in this city a man of God, and he is an honourable man; all that he saith cometh surely to pass: now let us go thither; peradventure he can shew us our way that we should go.

7 Then said Saul to his servant, But, behold, if we go, what shall we bring the man? for the bread is spent in our vessels, and there is not a present to bring to the man of God: what have we?

8 And the servant answered Saul again, and said, Behold, I have here at hand the fourth part of a shekel of silver: that will I give to the man of God, to tell us our way.

9 (Beforetime in Israel, when a man went to inquire of God, thus he spake, Come, and let us go to the seer: for he that is now called a Prophet was beforetime called a Seer.)

10 Then said Saul to his servant, Well said; come, let us go. So they went unto the city where the man of God was.

11 And as they went up the hill to the city, they found young maidens going out to draw water, and said unto them, Is the seer here?

12 And they answered them, and said, He is; behold, he is before you: make haste now, for he came to day to the city; for there is a sacrifice of the people to day in the high place:

13 As soon as ye be come into the city, ye shall straightway find him, before he go up to the high place to eat: for the people will not eat until he come, because he doth bless the sacrifice; and afterwards they eat that be bidden. Now therefore get you up; for about this time ye shall find him.

14 And they went up into the city: and when they were come into the city, behold, Samuel came out against them, for to go up to the high place.

15 Now the Lord had told Samuel in his ear a day before Saul came, saying,

16 To morrow about this time I will send thee a man out of the land of Benjamin, and thou shalt anoint him to be captain over my people Israel, that he may save my people out of the hand of the Philistines: for I have looked upon my people, because their cry is come unto me.

17 And when Samuel saw Saul, the Lord said unto him, Behold the man whom I spake to thee of! this same shall reign over my people.

18 Then Saul drew near to Samuel in the gate, and said, Tell me, I pray thee, where the seer's house is.

19 And Samuel answered Saul, and said, I am the seer: go up before me unto the high place; for ye shall eat with me to day, and to morrow I will let thee go, and will tell thee all that is in thine heart.

20 And as for thine asses that were lost three days ago, set not thy mind on them; for they are found. And on whom is all the desire of Israel? Is it not on thee, and on all thy father's house?

The scripture under reference captures the story of Saul. His father's asses were missing and he went in search of the asses in the company of his friend. As he went in search of the Asses, he came to three different places but the asses could not be found. He continued to search for the Asses until he got to a point where he almost gave up and began to worry over what his father would say. In his words, least our father forgets about the asses and start to think that we were missing so we should stop at this point. I want you to look at this story friends that even though the asses were missing, it was later restored by the God of restoration and that is what I believe will be happening to you when you pray the prayer in this book. Look at how Saul tried to restore the asses of his father by going to three different places, but he couldn't find the asses. I know that some of you may be thinking that you have tried and prayed and prayed for restoration to happen in your life. It may be possible that you have experienced a certain dimension of the grace of God in your life before, but now it seems as if it has all gone and things have dried up. And you've prayed and prayed. You have even sought the intercession of others, but it seems like nothing could be restored to you even though you have earnestly prayed. Know this, if an ass that was lost and searched for three days without the hope of finding anything, then your case is just a little thing. God who can restore animals can do much more by restoring your anointing and the grace that you have once enjoyed before now. This is a great possibility in God because God is a God of restoration both of time, things and bodies and even of human beings.

The moment Saul had an encounter with Samuel, what was missing was immediately restored to him because the God that we serve and worship is a God that restores what we have lost. The beauty of the prayer that you are going to be praying in this book is that it is in the courts of heaven and answers in the courts of heaven are faster and granted more speedily to God's children than when a believer prays conventional type of prayers.

The Souls

Luke 15:11-24

> *11 And he said, A certain man had two sons:*

> *12 And the younger of them said to his father, Father, give me the portion of goods*

that falleth to me. And he divided unto them his living.

13 And not many days after the younger son gathered all together, and took his journey into a far country, and there wasted his substance with riotous living.

14 And when he had spent all, there arose a mighty famine in that land; and he began to be in want.

15 And he went and joined himself to a citizen of that country; and he sent him into his fields to feed swine.

16 And he would fain have filled his belly with the husks that the swine did eat: and no man gave unto him.

17 And when he came to himself, he said, How many hired servants of my father's have bread enough and to spare, and I perish with hunger!

18 I will arise and go to my father, and will say unto him, Father, I have sinned against heaven, and before thee,

19 And am no more worthy to be called thy son: make me as one of thy hired servants.

20 And he arose, and came to his father. But when he was yet a great way off, his father saw him, and had compassion, and ran, and fell on his neck, and kissed him.

21 And the son said unto him, Father, I have sinned against heaven, and in thy sight, and am no more worthy to be called thy son.

22 But the father said to his servants, Bring forth the best robe, and put it on him; and put a ring on his hand, and shoes on his feet:

23 And bring hither the fatted calf, and kill it; and let us eat, and be merry:

24 For this my son was dead, and is alive again; he was lost, and is found. And they began to be merry.

The story of the prodigal son in this scripture which we have quoted above shows that restoration of souls is something that God does. This young man who was enjoying the protective covering of his father woke up one day and demanded all that belongs to him. He told his father that he should be given all that belongs to him. I have never seen a situation where a person was demanding the estate of his father while the father was still alive. The issue of inheritance comes to play when an individual is dead. It's only that time that the family begins to talk about sharing the inheritance of the person. But here, the prodigal son did the unthinkable for requesting for the father's estate when the father was alive. The young man went to a very far country and decided to engage in wasteful living by spending all that the father has given him on a lifestyle that was not befitting for a son that came out from such a home. But I want to say something very important here. That the Bible didn't tell us the number of years that this boy stayed while away from his father. It is possible that he spent ten years or even more. But the way the father received him should give us an idea that the son has been away for a very long time. The elaborate celebration which the father hosted for his son is indicative of the kind of time the boy was away from home. And the Bible tells us that he went to a far country and spent all the resources there. And in those days, their means of transportation is not like the one we have today. If you want to go to a very far place, you will probably spend days to get to that place or even months. This proves that the son has indeed been away from the arms of his loving father for a very long time. Yet he was restored to his father's arm. It doesn't matter how long what you have lost, it will be restored to you in the courts of heaven. If a human being can be restored, then your finances or other things that you have lost is a small thing. The Bible says this is but a light thing before the eyes of the Lord.

Job's Life

The story of the life of Job is a typical example that our God is a God of restoration. The Bible tells us that job is the richest man in the East.

Job 1:1-3

> *There was a man in the land of Uz, whose name was Job; and that man was perfect and upright, and one that feared God, and eschewed evil.*
>
> *2 And there were born unto him seven sons and three daughters.*
>
> *3 His substance also was seven thousand sheep, and three thousand camels, and five hundred yoke of oxen, and five hundred she asses, and a very great household; so that this man was the greatest of all the men of the east.*

Not only was he rich, but Job was also able to combine his wealth with a solid level of spirituality. This is why the Bible says in the book of Job, that I have made a covenant with my eyes not to look at a woman lustfully. It was from this righteous background that Job came from. He was the greatest man in the land of Uz. He had so much wealth that in the East, nobody could be compared with him. Not only was Job having a lot of wealth, but he was also using his resources for the enlargement of the kingdom of God by helping the poor and needy. When the devil discovered that the impact that Job was making with his wealth was too much, he sought permission from God to attack the life of Job. This was a man who has everything but after the attack of the devil upon his life, he came back to level zero. The attack was so much that even his wife who was standing by him all these years and enjoying the blessedness of the resources that God has entrusted into the hands of Job, enticed him to curse God so that he would die. Job sharply rejected the advice of his wife. And he rebuked her for speaking like a foolish woman. Job lost everything he had. He had seven sons and daughters, but all of them were gone. He had three thousand camels, five thousand yokes of oxen, and five hundred she asses, and his household was great.

Job 42:12-13

> *So the Lord blessed the latter end of Job more than his beginning: for he had fourteen thousand sheep, and six thousand camels, and a thousand yoke of oxen, and a thousand she asses.*
>
> *He had also seven sons and three daughters.*

After God permitted the devil to tempt Job, everything that he had was gone. What is so interesting about this story of Job is that there was a time that one of the servants of Job came and told him that the fire of God came down from heaven and consumed your sheep.

I want you to look carefully at what I'm about to tell you that is where you will know that our God is a God of restoration. And whatever you have lost, he can give you back.

In the Scripture under reference that we have just mentioned, not only did God restore the things that Job lost, God also doubled everything that he had before. For the Lord was able to give him twice as much as he had before the attack of the devil upon his life and his financial resources. You can imagine what Job went through for a man who was the greatest man in the East to lose that position that he held and came back to level zero. And if God can restore the life of Job in this manner, then yours is a very small thing before his eyes. There is nothing that God can't restore to you which is why this topic was carefully named in this chapter as walking with the God of restoration. It doesn't matter what you have lost provided you are connected to the God of restoration, everything will be given back to you either in the same measure that you have before or even in a greater way as it happened to the life of Job.

Friends, I am drawing the scriptural examples to paint a clear picture in your mind concerning the God of restoration and what can be done in the courts of heaven when you go before God. Whatever it is that is gone, can be brought back. We don't know how long the affliction of Job lasted, and we also don't know how long the loss of his financial resources endured. However, what we can see from the Scripture is that God gave everything back to Job in a greater measure. Is it anointing? Is it glory? Grace? Financial resources? Health? Anything at all that you have lost I want you to understand that the God of restoration can do so for you in the Courts of Heaven. And if he can make restoration for you in the Courts of Heaven, everything that you once had will be restored to you. That is the kind of picture I want you to have in your mind while praying in the courts of heaven for restoration.

If God can take a man who was on the ground level to the upper level, the place where he once occupied gloriously then your case is a small one, and I know that when you are going to the courts of heaven to pray for the restoration of the things that you have lost, it will be done for you in the name of Jesus. The Bible tells us that we can have hope through the comfort of the Scripture. So if God can do it in the time of Job, the Bible further says that the God who did it in the time of Job is still the same yesterday, today, and forever. If he did it before, he can do it again and again.

Friends that is the God of restoration and how he was able to bring back the life of Job to the place where it was.

And I trust him that he will do so for you too. The example in Scripture which we have seen of the life of Job typifies the situation where God can restore a human being. And if God can restore a human being, then things and properties can be restored too. If only you can pray the right way in the Courts of Heaven for the restoration of the things that you have lost then you will get everything back and even greater.

If you saw what happened in the life of Job if you were physically there when he was undergoing that kind of experience as a result of the attack of the devil upon his life you never had thought that God will be able to bring back all that he had lost. The situation in the life of Job was so hopeless that even his friends who are supposed to be comforting him, began to speak carelessly concerning him, some even accusing him of doing something wrong. But a single encounter with the God of restoration turned everything around for Job.

So, we have seen from our illustration so far that our God can restore human beings, things, and even souls. By the time you begin to pray in the Courts of Heaven for restoration, this is the kind of picture you should have in your mind. Scriptural examples can impart your faith to believe God for the impossible. The Bible tells us that these things were written for our example. From the Scriptural example, we can see that this is what God did in the life of this person, and I know that as a result of the fact that he did it in the life of another, in time past, he can still do it in my life again. That is what the Scripture does to the life of a believer by generating faith for God to do what is impossible for the mortal mind to comprehend.

The coins

Although this is a parable in the Scripture, it illustrates to us the extent of the restoration that God can make in the life of a believer.

Luke 15:8-9

> *Either what woman having ten pieces of silver, if she lose one piece, doth not light a candle, and sweep the house, and seek diligently till she find it?*
>
> *9 And when she hath found it, she calleth her friends and her neighbours together, saying, Rejoice with me; for I have found the piece which I had lost.*

The Bible tells us of the woman who had lost her coin, and she immediately went in search of that coin. She turned on the light, looked for it in different places until she had found the coin. The moment she found the coin, she called for a celebration and threw a big party in the neighbourhood because of the coin that she had found. Everyone including her friends and neighbours gathered together to celebrate with her because of her finding. And you know what she was telling everybody when they gathered for the party? This was a coin that I lost, but now I have found it. Everything seemed to be shocking to this woman when she discovered that her coin which was lost and without hope was found.

And do you know what the story in the Bible tells you if you have lost financial resources before God can restore them to you? It is possible that at that time you were careless concerning the resources that God has entrusted into your hands and as a result of your actions, you lose all the financial resources that you had. Well, you can ask God for mercy and God will restore all that you have lost. That is the type of God that we serve. He is a God of restoration and he can bring back all that the enemy has taken from you including what you have lost as a result of carelessness on your part when you have asked him for mercy.

Friends, the Scripture that we have seen above tells us that God can restore things that have been lost. It was just a coin that was missing, it was restored to the woman, and the moment she found it, there was a celebration. I believe God for you too that as you go into the courts of heaven to pray for the restoration of the things that you have lost, God will respond by issuing an order from the courts of heaven for the restoration of that thing and because of the restoration that God will perform in your life, many will gather to celebrate with you in the name of Jesus. There is a kind of miracle that God can give that commands the attention of people whether they like it or not. There is a type of blessing that God can give that can command the attention of people irrespective of the fact that they don't want to care. This is something that you need to understand my friends that if God wants to make restoration in the life of a person he does a complete restoration. The Bible tells us that God will restore unto you all the years that the caterpillar and the cankerworms have eaten. So this is a complete restoration that God is talking about it isn't partial at all. In the same way that this woman did not find a part of the coin somewhere, what she found was the complete coin and as a result of that, there was a celebration in the neighbourhood. I pray today that as you go to the courts of heaven to pray for the restoration of the things that you have lost, you will get them back in the name of Jesus.

The Body

Jeremiah 30:17

> *For I will restore health unto thee, and I will heal thee of thy wounds, saith the Lord; because they called thee an Outcast, saying, This is Zion, whom no man seeketh after.*

In the Scripture that we have just quoted above, we can see the assurance of God that he will restore healing and health to us. Now, this is another aspect of restoration that God can effect on the body of an individual. I told you that when you are dealing with the God of restoration in the Courts of Heaven, except that everything is possible. It may be possible that your health may be suffering right now even though this was not the way it used to be. It was surprising too that you just woke up one morning and started to battle with this affliction on your body. You did not know where it came from and how it came into your body. It is now a reality that you are battling with every day of your life and you are astounded. If that is your case, I want you to know that the God of restoration will bring back your health to the place it used to be before the attack of the enemy upon your body.

God even knew that it was possible for the health of a person to be lost. This is why the Scripture says, I will restore. You can only restore something that has either been damaged, or is no longer the way it used to be. God works a restoration so that what you used to enjoy before can be enjoyed now. Several people in the Bible lost their health and had it restored through the healing power of God. The closest example that I will give to you is the woman with the issue of blood. She was not a child, but she had been battling with that affliction for 18 years of her life. Before those 18 years, the woman was okay. What happened to her? She lost her health. A need for restoration of the health that she had lost became apparent. One single encounter with the God of restoration, Jesus, dissolved that affliction of 18 years that had been bothering her.

In my personal life, I have had situations where God has to do a restoration upon my health. In 2019, sometimes in August, I suffered from an affliction called irritable bowel syndrome. The affliction was so intense that I wondered what was happening to me. Before August, I was doing okay. But immediately when that August came, everything changed. Any time I ate something, I had a digestion problem, and I was always rushing into the toilet. If by mistake I eat anything spicy, my bowel would move, and I will have severe diarrhoea. I lose so much weight and I was also losing vital nutrients in my body including the zinc level. It was so severe that I became anxious over what was happening to my health. It was then that I began to appreciate some of the little things that we take for granted such as when you eat food and you do not have any digestion problem. I went to the hospital for a medical examination. The doctor had to even conduct an HIV test on me. But of course, the results were negative. After a thorough examination of my body, he prescribed drugs and urged me to continue to take them. I came home and began to take the drugs as prescribed by the doctor. But the more I took the drugs, the more I look sick. But amid that affliction, the

Lord kept assuring me that he would heal me. Looking back at the events that transpired, everything at that time looked impossible because of my condition. But by the grace of God, I am healed completely because the God of restoration has restored my health. If God can do it in my life, he can do it in yours also. The Bible tells us that the testimony of Jesus is the spirit of prophecy. Anything that you have seen God has done in the life of another, is a message to you that he can do it in yours too.

You may be reading this right now with a medical condition or a report that the doctor has handed over to you. To drive down fear into your spine, the doctor even told you that there is nothing that can be done about the condition. I don't blame the doctor, he is speaking based on his experience as a medical practitioner. Neither do I condemn him he's doing his job. However, there is an aspect of restoration in the Courts of Heaven which the medical doctor has not encountered. And that is what is going to be happening to you today. You don't need two encounters, just one encounter with the God of restoration in the courts of heaven will settle the medical condition forever. I have had countless testimonies of brothers and sisters in the Lord who had battled with one form of affliction or the other, but today their health has been completely restored. So whenever you are going to the Courts of Heaven for Courts of Heaven prayers for the restoration of your health, let your heart stay on this fact that the same God who has been able to restore the health of others will do so to you.

Seasons and Times

The story of Hannah in the Bible left us with much to be desired. The husband married two wives. One of the wives is Penninah and the other Hannah. While Penninah had children, Hannah had no children. Penninah decided to make the point of her having children something she was using to mock Hannah to the point that Hannah became so depressed and wanted to kill herself with starvation. When the husband saw it was too much he called her attention to her mood, by saying Hannah, why are you weeping, Am I not better to you than ten sons? But the words of the husband meant nothing to Hannah who was too depressed to appreciate the encouraging words of her husband. Penninah continued that way to harass Hannah with her childlessness until Hannah could not take it anymore. Since she was so troubled down to her marrow, and she has nowhere to lay her burden, she took it to the Lord in the place of prayer during Shiloh one year. The way that her adversary provoked her was reflected in the way that she poured her heart to the Lord. When Eli the priest saw her praying to the Lord on that day during Shiloh, he concluded her for a drunk woman who came to Shiloh to display her drunkenness. She was bold enough to tell the man of God that she was not drunk but that she was burdened by what has besieged her life, and she wanted to pour out her heart to the Lord who can turn around her story. When the man of God realised that she was not drunken, he joined his faith with her faith and said, may the Lord grant you the petition that you have asked of him. The moment Hannah heard the prophetic declaration of the man of God, she decided to act in faith by standing up from the place of prayer and drying up her tears. She went home and the food that she refused to eat, she began to eat and the sad and depressive expression that clung to her face disappeared. After that encounter with Eli the man of God at Shiloh, something happened to Hannah. The Bible never told us that Penninah stopped mocking her. However, something about Hannah changed because she knew that God has answered. No matter what Penninah did going forward never bothered her and because she changed attitude, her tears were wiped away. She gave birth to a son, Samuel who became a great prophet in the land of Israel. His prophetic grace was strong that all Israel knew that the Lord has established Samuel to be a prophet of the Lord. And when he started to prophesy over the people of the land of Israel, the Bible says none of his words fell to the ground.

The question is, did any restoration happened in the life of Hannah? Yes, God restored all the times and seasons that she had lost by giving her seven children. And one of the children that she gave birth to had so much relevance in Israel and reckoned as one of the great prophets in the land of Israel. In the whole of the land of Israel, there was nowhere that the children of Penninah were mentioned. They all died as nonentities, unknown by any means while the one that she was mocking almost all the time had a son that his relevance as a prophet of the Lord is being mentioned till today.

Hannah even said that she that'd many children has become feeble. When we talk about the ability of God to make restoration in the life of a believer, this is what we mean. As I am speaking to you right now, there may be seasons in your life that you have missed. It is also possible that there are times in your life when you thought that some things were going to happen, but you don't know how you missed it. You are dealing with God who can restore seasons and times. If he did it in the life of Hannah, he can do it in your life because the Bible tells us that God is the same yesterday today and forever.

Even in the life of Sarah the wife of Abraham, God restored to her the seasons of her life that she had missed. Some people might say that this is not a testimony, how can she give birth to a child at her old age. Well, it depends on the way you are looking at it. Is it not better to give birth to a child who can become something in life, than one who is a nonentity? You hear people mention the God of Abraham, the God of Isaac and the God of Jacob. It was Sarah who gave birth to a son who became one of the progenitors of the saints today. It was through him that the blessing was passed to many generations. The beauty of restoration of times and season is that whenever God wants to restore times and seasons that you have missed or lost as a result of the attack of the enemy, he does not restore it in the exact way you missed it. If a favour was supposed to enter into your hands that you missed at a season of your life, God has the power to restore it to you in a different season. For example, if the favour was supposed to bring something that will change your life when God is making a restoration he does not do it in the exact form that you lost it. He doubles it, just as we saw in the life of Job. What is it that you have lost at certain seasons and times of your life that you have been mourning and regretting over? The God that we serve can restore to you the seasons of life that you have missed even if that attack was as a result of your carelessness, if you ask for mercy, God will restore to you those times and seasons that you have lost. When I speak about carelessness, I am talking about being foolish about the seasons and times of your life. For some people, the Lord may have used someone as a gate for the next level of your life, but you took the person the Lord was using for granted and that gate was closed. As a result of that, the next level couldn't be achieved. I want to let you know that the reason why we call God the merciful God is that he can restore to you what you have lost out of your fault. Am I saying that we should be careless because God can restore the things that we have lost? Of course, not! Why would I do so?

Friends, whenever you hear me talking about restoration in the Courts of Heaven that is what I mean. That God will not only restore to you things that you have lost but also seasons and times of your life that have been lost either as a result of the mistake that you have made or due to the attack of the enemy upon your life. Instead of crying over the missed opportunities of your life which opened in certain seasons, why not begin to praise God because restoration is about to happen to you now.

CHAPTER 3

Why the Courts of Heaven Prayers for Restoration

Someone may be asking, brother Pius, but I can pray this type of prayer anywhere, and God will hear and answer me. You are correct. Scripturally, the Bible tells us that this is the confidence we have in him when we pray in accordance with his will, he hears us. But there is something different about praying in the Courts of Heaven for restoration. And I am going to be showing you some of these things so that you would pray in the courts of heaven and see results.

The presence

God is everywhere the Bible tells us and so is his presence. But one of the greatest places where the concentration of the power and presence of God can ever be experienced is in the Courts of Heaven. God carries out all his administrative activities of the earth and the heavens in the courts. And it is for this reason that the power and the presence of God will be felt in greater dimension in the Courts of Heaven. And whenever the presence of God is available, restoration has been made a lot easier. If the presence of God that came down upon the mountain of Sinai was so intense that even the children of Israelites had to beg Moses to go and hear God on their behalf, then imagine what will happen if you come before the courts of heaven with the highest concentration of the presence of God? It is for this reason why it is better to pray in the courts of heaven for restoration than to pray in any other place. It is not that if you decide to pray this prayer in other places God will not answer you, but there is nothing as powerful as praying in the presence of God in his courts.

1 Kings 19:11-12

> *And he said, Go forth, and stand upon the mount before the Lord. And, behold, the Lord passed by, and a great and strong wind rent the mountains, and brake in pieces the rocks before the Lord; but the Lord was not in the wind: and after the wind an earthquake; but the Lord was not in the earthquake:*
>
> *12 And after the earthquake a fire; but the Lord was not in the fire: and after the fire a still small voice.*

Elijah had an experience with the presence of God, and he was astounded. He thought that God was in the fire, but he was not. He also thought that God was in the earthquake, but God was not. What was it that was causing the earthquake and what was it that was causing the fire? The answer is simple, the presence of God. If an angel of God could carry the presence of God in such a way that he can put one of his legs in the sea and the other on the dry land, how much more will you experience when you come before the God that gave the power to the angel?

Friends is not that you can't pray this type of prayer for restoration anywhere. You can. But you are in a better position when you pray in the courts of heaven because the courts of heaven contain the presence of God in such an unimaginable way that when it meets your request for restoration, answers are imminent. Look at all the people in the Bible who had an encounter with the presence of the Lord. What happened to them? Moses had been running away from pharaoh all his life as a result of the Egyptian which he had killed. But the simple encounter with the presence of the Lord in a burning bush transformed Moses the fearful to Moses the bold. It was the same Pharaoh who had been chasing him that Moses returned with the power of the presence of the Lord to confront.

It wasn't that something different happened to Moses. But it was just that encounter he had in the presence of the Lord that killed the fear that Moses had for the King of Egypt. The same Moses went back after those who were seeking to kill him and started saying to them, thus says the Lord, let my people go that they may serve me. What changed the tone of Moses from fearful to bold? The presence of the Lord. He went to Egypt on the strength of the presence of the Lord which he saw in the burning Bush and conquered it. The manifestation that followed were too great that when the King of Egypt saw it was too much, he had to cry to Moses for help. Even the elders of Egypt joined the voices of those calling for the release of the Israelites from the land of Egypt. They came to the King of Egypt and said let them go that they may serve the Lord, are you not seeing that the land of Egypt has been destroyed? One man came, saw Egypt, and conquered it because he had an encounter with the presence of the Lord in the burning bush. You may not be encountering the presence of the Lord in the burning Bush as Moses did, you are encountering the presence of the Lord in the Courts of Heaven. Will you see a physical fire as Moses saw in the backside of the desert? No! Yours is by faith! Something more tangible than even what Moses saw in the burning bush. The Bible says by faith we understand that the world was framed up so that what we are seeing today appeared from nowhere. Yes, you heard me. Nowhere. My prayer for you is this, as you go into the courts of heaven to pray for restoration, the presence of God you will meet in the highest concentrated form will cause a full restoration of all that you have lost in the name of Jesus.

Joseph

The story of Joseph in the Bible is a popular one but I want to use it and draw your attention to some things that he was able to achieve in his life. We all know from scripture that Joseph was a child of many colours, signifying how glorious his destiny would be.

Genesis 37:3-7

> *Now Israel loved Joseph more than all his children, because he was the son of his old age: and he made him a coat of many colours.*
>
> *4 And when his brethren saw that their father loved him more than all his brethren, they hated him, and could not speak peaceably unto him.*
>
> *5 And Joseph dreamed a dream, and he told it his brethren: and they hated him yet the more.*
>
> *6 And he said unto them, Hear, I pray you, this dream which I have dreamed:*

> *7 For, behold, we were binding sheaves in the field, and, lo, my sheaf arose, and also stood upright; and, behold, your sheaves stood round about, and made obeisance to my sheaf.*

He started by reporting his brothers for their evil deeds which they had been doing. In addition to that, the dream that Joseph had made them hate him severely. But you know it doesn't matter who is hating on you provided God is showering you with love. It doesn't matter those who don't want to see you provided God is with you and for you. Despite all the wars of hatred that Joseph's brethren heaped on his head, he went on to become one of the most successful men in the land of Egypt. The brothers of Joseph cast him into a well. But do you know who was with Joseph? The presence of the Lord. Imagine what happened, they cast him into the well. Not that they lowered him into the well. He was cast into the well. No injury was sustained. No broken bones. And with the way that his brothers were angry with him, you know that they may have thrown him into the well with intense anger. Yet in all this throwing, nothing happened to Joseph.

Friends, sometimes when you see people conspiring against you, you become afraid thinking that the conspiracy is going to work and prevent you from enjoying the kind of life that God has ordained for you.

But I can tell you that just as God preserved Joseph when his enemies cast him into the well, that is how God preserves from every trap that the enemy has set for you. Even if God allowed the conspiracy to come to pass, it will not still affect your life. If the presence of the Lord was able to preserve Joseph, then it will preserve you too. No matter the plans of the enemy against your life, it will never work because the presence of the Lord is with you.

And the Lord can't be with a person without the presence of the Lord been there. The Bible tells us that the Lord was with Joseph. As a result of the fact that the Lord was with Joseph, everything around his life was prospering including the house of Potiphar his new adopted master. The blessings of the Lord upon the house of Potiphar was so tremendous that the man did not care about anything at all except the food that he ate.

Genesis 39:5-6

> *And it came to pass from the time that he had made him overseer in his house, and over all that he had, that the Lord blessed the Egyptian's house for Joseph's sake; and the blessing of the Lord was upon all that he had in the house, and in the field.*
>
> *6 And he left all that he had in Joseph's hand; and he knew not ought he had, save*

*the bread which he did eat. And Joseph was
a goodly person, and well favoured.*

Joseph was such a man with the presence of the Lord. Egypt was saved from the destruction that may have come through starvation as a result of the presence of the Lord with one man, Joseph. If not for the presence of the Lord around the life of Joseph, his brothers would have perished from starvation too. Joseph heavily enjoyed the presence of the Lord. There is power in the presence of the Lord that can cause a restoration to happen in the life of a believer, and if Joseph was able to enjoy an overwhelming power of the presence of the Lord, which caused a lot of things to happen to him, then you are going directly into the courts of heaven to pray for the presence of God which is experienced in the highest form will change your life also.

Elijah

1 Kings 18:46

>*And the hand of the Lord was on Elijah; and
>he girded up his loins, and ran before Ahab
>to the entrance of Jezreel.*

In the life of this man, we saw a demonstration of the power of the presence of God in the life of a person. The Bible tells us that the presence of God was upon the life of Elijah that he outran the chariots of Ahab. If you look closely at the rendition of that verse, you will not see the word presence of the Lord in the place. You will only see the word the hand of the Lord came upon Elijah, and he outran the chariot of Ahab. We have already stated that the presence of the Lord can't be separated from God. Anywhere God is, his presence is there too. In essence, it was the presence of the Lord that came upon the life of Elijah that he was able to outrun the chariot of Ahab. Now you are going into the courts of heaven to experience the power of his presence why would a restoration not take place in your life? That is impossible.

Daniel

Daniel 6:17

> *And a stone was brought and laid upon the mouth of the den; and the king sealed it with his own signet, and with the signet of his lords; that the purpose might not be changed concerning Daniel.*

It was God who sent an angel on a specific mission of shutting down the lion's mouth so that Daniel wouldn't be hurt. But those angels didn't come from Jupiter or Mars. They came from the presence of the Lord, and the power of that presence has the capacity of shutting the mouth of the lions. When the King came in the morning to know if the Lord had delivered Daniel, he said has the Lord which you serve continually able to deliver you?

Daniel's answer was a straight yes. We know that the angels came from the presence of the Lord because when Gabriel wanted to introduce himself to Zachariah, he said Gabriel that stands in the presence of the Lord.

Luke 1:19

> *And the angel answering said unto him, I am Gabriel, that stand in the presence of God; and am sent to speak unto thee, and to shew thee these glad tidings.*

And I pray that the same presence of the Lord will cause the tremendous restoration to happen in your life in the name of Jesus.

Power

Why should you pray for restoration in the courts of heaven? The answer is that power compels the performance of an action. People obey the government of their country because the government has power and authority. Power has been defined as the ability to compel the performance of an action or do work. What work? The work of restoration in your life and destiny of course. What is it that you have lost? The power of the presence of God in the Courts of Heaven can compel the restoration of what you desire. The Bible says in the days of his power, the people shall be willing. People's willingness is compelled by the power of God's presence.

Let me show you an example in the Scripture of the power of God's presence.

Speed

We have said earlier that the presence of the Lord cannot be separated from the Lord himself. Whenever you hear the word the presence of the Lord, it means that God himself is there that is something we have already established. We saw in the book of 1 Kings 18 how the hand of the Lord came upon the life of Elijah, and he outran the chariot of Ahab. What was it that came upon the life of Elijah that made him overtake the chariot of Ahab? The presence of the Lord. Anywhere the presence of the Lord is, there is a limitless possibility. If God is in any environment, anything can happen as a result of his presence there. There is nothing that gives you supernatural speed like praying in the courts of heaven. This is as a result of the concentrated and tangible presence of God available there. And we have said earlier that the presence of the Lord in its concentrated form can be felt in the Courts of Heaven. So whenever you go to pray in the courts of heaven, you are getting in touch with the presence of God that will allocate you divine speed. Which is the reason why answers in the courts of heaven are faster than when you pray conventional prayers. That is the power of praying in the courts of heaven because of the presence of the Lord. And I pray for you today, as you go into the courts of heaven to pray for restoration over your life and destiny or anything that has been lost in your life, you will experience divine speed in the name of Jesus.

CHAPTER 4

Entering the Courts to meet the God of Restoration

Before you begin praying in the courts of heaven for the restoration of anything in your life, the first thing that you need to do is to enter into the courts of heaven. To do that, there are procedures for entrance into the courts of heaven. And unless you follow the procedure for entering into the courts of heaven, any prayer that you pray outside the courts won't be effective as the prayer that was prayed in the courts of heaven.

The Blood

The Blood of Jesus was not given to us for our redemption alone, it was also given for our purification. The Bible says without the blood of Jesus there can't be any forgiveness of sins. The blood of Jesus is the only ground upon which we can enter into the holies of holy and the courts of heaven to offer our prayers. To this end, before you begin praying in the courts of heaven, ensure that you apply the blood directly to your life. And you do this by pleading the blood of Jesus over your life. In any area of your life that you have sinned against God, you need to ask him for mercies so that the blood can cleanse and wash you from that sin. The Bible says that we should come boldly before the throne of grace that we may find help and grace in the time of need. Do you know that any time that you come before the Lord asking for mercy, you are indeed making demands for the blood of Jesus to come and intervene for you? The blood of Jesus can both wash and cleanse you before you begin your courts of heaven prayer session. Employ the use of the blood of Jesus for your washing and purification. This is the first step towards entering into the courts of heaven. The Bible tells us that the eyes of the Lord are too holy to behold iniquity and if his eyes are too holy to see what is unclean and sinful then that same sin can't come before his courts and request for restoration of any kind.

Invite the Holy Spirit

After making demands for the blood of Jesus to cleanse and purify you from whatever that you have done, the next thing that you need to do is to invite the Holy Spirit. I will be very blunt and frank with you, that without the ministry and the help of the Holy Spirit, it may be impossible to pray effectively in the courts of heaven for restoration and see results. The Bible tells us that the

Holy Spirit will convict the world of sin and judgment too. Do you remember when you did something or said something you ought not to say and you felt the conviction of the Holy Spirit in your heart rebuking you that what you said was not proper in the circumstance? It may be that what you said wasn't even a sin, but something that the right time to say wasn't ripe or you ought not to have said what you said. And the Holy Spirit instantly performed his ministry of conviction by letting you know straight that you should not talk or say things like that. What the Holy Spirit is doing there is to ensure that you are aligned with God. He knows that there are things that you can say or do which can take you out of alignment with the Lord so he's rebuking you for you to make amends so that your prayers will be very effective any day, any time.

Alignment is the rightness of the heart with the Lord in every area of your life. If you can always keep your heart and your life aligned, the power that your prayers can generate will amaze you.

Friends, before you go into the courts of heaven to pray for the restoration of anything, ensure that you call on the Holy Spirit to come and then pray that the Holy Spirit, will help you to get aligned with God in all areas of your life. The moment you do and he aligned your heart, your prayers in the courts of heaven for restoration will be potent and effective. These are some of the secrets of prayer men and women that pray all the time and see results.

Faith it Process

One of the essential needs of the life of the believer for life and destiny is called faith. In the book of Hebrews 11:6, the Bible says that if we don't have faith, we can't please God or make him happy. So we need faith to operate in the realm of the spirit and the realm of the earth. Except the person isn't a believer that is when he will be free to operate by his senses. But as a child of God, faith is necessary for your walk with the Lord and for you to take possession of that which belongs to you. In the Hall of Faith, the Bible enumerated several men and women of faith who were able to make things happen as a result of their faith in God. The Bible says some of these people shut the mouths of lions, conquered the enemy and destroyed all the barriers that stood in their way.

Hebrews 11:34

> *Quenched the violence of fire, escaped the edge of the sword, out of weakness were made strong, waxed valiant in fight, turned to flight the armies of the aliens.*

Someone may think that I entered into the courts of heaven, and I didn't feel anything. The truth is that we as children of God don't walk by feelings but by faith.

Sometimes we don't feel like doing certain things but nevertheless, do it because the Holy Spirit wants it done or the word has already commanded us that we should do it. The truth is, if you become a master of your feelings, it may be impossible for you to achieve anything in life. The Bible says he that regards the wind or the rain my not sow and reap.

When it comes to praying in the courts of heaven, your faith is required. You may not see or feel anything but once you have been able to follow the procedure for gaining access into the courts of heaven, then you are there. Don't be a master of your feelings, but a master of your faith.

Presenter Procedure

If I tell you today that you are to meet the president of the United States for dinner, how would you package yourself? Will you dress in rags to appear before one of the strongest presidents of the world? Will you carelessly come before the president? Are you going to come before the president in the way that you feel like? I am leaving you to answer all of these questions. But I am sure that you won't come before the President of the U.S in that manner. If you won't come before an earthly man like that, how can you come before the Lord, the Kings of Kings, the one that the Bible says, knows the place where the foundation of the earth sank, Jehovah Jireh and Rafa. The manner you come before the courts of heaven and your entering procedure determines whether you can gain access into the courts of heaven. Put yourself together. Put your distractions away from your life. You can't have your phone ringing while you are before the courts of heaven. You put yourself together like a man who is appearing before the highest King. If you don't present yourself well, it is possible not to have access to the courts of heaven where your prayers for restoration will be offered.

Friends, the courts of heaven is a great place where prayers are offered. And when you come before the courts of heaven, where God administers the things of the earth and the things that pertain to heaven, then you need to package yourself and present yourself well before the throne of Grace. No defiled robes should be entertained there.

CHAPTER 5

Prayer Section

Prayer for session A

We have come to an important aspect of this book that deals with prayer, if there is anything that has the capacity of distracting you right now, I want you to put it away. In that way, nothing will be able to take your focus off the prayer. You don't read prayers, you get on your feet and pray them into fulfilment. In this section of the prayer, we shall be dealing with the restoration of physical things in the next section of the prayer, which is B, we shall be dealing with the spiritual aspect of restoration that deals with your life and destiny on the earth.

Prayer for Restoration of the Body and Health

This prayer is for those who once enjoyed divine health but suddenly lost it as a result of either the attack of the enemy or physical infirmity that may be caused by diseases. In the book of Jeremiah 30:17, the Bible made it clear to us that our God can restore our health. To restore is to bring back something to the state it was before the occurrence of an event. That event could be the attack of the enemy or infirmities that were caused as a result of certain natural elements. Whatever the circumstances of that situation, God can restore your health to the place it was before that incident. If you have woken up one day suddenly to discover that the activities of life that you were enjoying have become impossible due to the attack of the enemy upon your health, the God of restoration in the courts of heaven can bring back your health to you. Some people have been enjoying good health but the enemy lay siege upon their health. They were enjoying the divine life that God has given to them but the enemy came and planted the seed of ill-health in their lives. From that point, a liability existence began. They have become a burden both to their family and loved ones. If that is your experience, I want to assure you that the God of restoration in the courts of heaven will restore your health to you in the name of Jesus.

Reflection

Jeremiah 30:17

For I will restore health unto thee, and I will heal thee of thy wounds, saith the Lord; because they called thee an Outcast, saying, This is Zion, whom no man seeketh after.

Malachi 4:2

But unto you that fear my name shall the Sun of righteousness arise with healing in his wings; and ye shall go forth, and grow up as calves of the stall.

Prayer

Holy Father, I want to thank you for the privileged that you have given me to come before the Courts of Heaven at this hour. I am not taking this opportunity and privilege for granted, I am very grateful in the name of Jesus.

Heavenly Father, I come before your courts today to ask for mercy that if this ill-health is as a result of the door I have opened to the enemy, I ask today that let your mercy prevail over every justified attack of the enemy upon my health in the name of Jesus.

Holy Father, every arrow of infirmity that has been fired from the pit of hell against my life and destiny, today before your courts of heaven that arrow is fired back to where it came from in the name of Jesus.

Gracious Father, by the power of your presence that brings great deliverance upon the life of your people, and I have come before your courts to enjoy the concentrated power of your presence, let the healing virtue flow from the crown of my head down to the soles of my feet in the name of Jesus.

Heavenly Father, I have seen from your word that you are a God of restoration that can give me the health that I have been enjoying before the attack of the enemy upon my life, I ask today before the courts of heaven that a restoration order for my health be issued for my sake and let me begin to enjoy the health I used to enjoy before the attack of the enemy upon my body in the name of Jesus.

Holy Father, I know that no limitation can hold me bound in your presence and your word has also said that the anointing breaks every yoke. I've come in contact with the anointed presence in your courts and by the virtue of that presence let the yoke of infirmity that has been upon my body be broken in the name of Jesus.

Righteous Father, if the infirmity that has come upon my body is as a result of witchcraft work, I pray today that from your courts right now the same people who did that witchcraft attack will receive a double portion of that infirmity upon their lives right now in the name of Jesus.

Holy Father, I have seen from your word that the blood of Jesus has already purchased my healing and deliverance from the spirit of infirmity. I pray today before your courts that the power of the blood of Jesus causes a full restoration of my health right now in the name of Jesus.

Holy Father, you have said in your word that the Sun of righteousness will arise with healing in his wings. I pray today that as the Sun of righteousness arises with healing in his wings, a restoration of my health will immediately happen in the name of Jesus.

Glorious Father, I have also seen from your word that he that digs a pit will fall into it. He that rolls a stone, it will come upon him. Anyone responsible for this attack of sickness on my body, I make demands before your courts of heaven at this hour that beyond the restoration you will do upon my body, that infirmity returns to whoever that sent it in the name of Jesus.

Heavenly Father, You have said in your word that a sword cannot devour forever. No matter how powerful this infirmity has been upon my body, today it has come to its end before your courts. A full restoration must take place in my life and this infirmity will never come back in the name of Jesus.

Holy Father, I have seen from your word that you've carried all my infirmity and upon you was all my chastisement laid. I make demands upon the Scripture right now before your courts of heaven, and I ask that all the benefits of redemption that have been purchased by your blood for my sake be made manifest upon my body right now in the name of Jesus.

Thank you, Lord, for hearing and answering my prayers for restoration of my health in the Courts of Heaven to you be all the glory and the honour in the name of Jesus.

Financial Restoration

If you have been enjoying financial blessings before and all of a sudden you crashed to the ground, and you are wondering what has happened to you provided that you didn't make any mistakes concerning the finances that God has entrusted into your hands, then you need this prayer for the restoration of your finances in the Courts of Heaven. It doesn't matter what aspect of your finances seemed to be lost, the God of restoration in the courts of heaven has the power to restore your financial status. This is where many believers have found themselves after enjoying financial abundance, they are now struggling. It is not the will of the Lord for a believer to be up today, and be down tomorrow.

Proverbs 4:18

But the path of the just is as the shining light, that shineth more and more unto the perfect day.

The Bible tells us that the path of the just is as shiny light that continues to shine unto the perfect day. It is not the will of God for your yesterday, to be better than your today. It is contrary to biblical principles and standards. So if you have been enjoying financial abundance yesterday, and today it is no more you need financial restoration in the Courts of Heaven.

Friends, I know that as you are currently reading the pages of this book right now, the eyes of your heart is beginning to get enlightened that you need financial restoration. That you are struggling now, it is not the will of God. What God does in the life of a believer is an enduring blessing. If you look at the life of Abraham, the Bible says he was rich in silver, cattle, and gold (Genesis 13:2). As a result of that enduring blessing that was upon his life, it was passed on to Isaac, and even unto Jacob and all of his children.

Genesis 25:5-6

And Abraham gave all that he had unto Isaac.

6 But unto the sons of the concubines, which Abraham had, Abraham gave gifts, and sent them away from Isaac his son, while he yet lived, eastward, unto the east country.

That is the kind of blessing that the Lord pours upon the lives of his people. And I pray that as you go into the courts of heaven, any financial restoration that you need will be done in accordance with the will of God in the name of Jesus.

Reflection

Proverbs 10:22

> *The blessing of the Lord, it maketh rich, and he addeth no sorrow with it.*

Philippians 4:19

> *But my God shall supply all your need according to his riches in glory by Christ Jesus.*

Prayer

Holy Father, let your name be praised and be honoured for the privilege and opportunity that your mighty hand has granted to me to come before your courts at this hour to pray for the restoration of my finances to you be all the glory and the honour in the name of Jesus.

Holy Father, I come before your courts at this hour to make demands for your mercy since the financial loss that has happened in my life was as a result of my carelessness or mistakes, I pray that you will show me your mercy before the courts of heaven right now in the name of Jesus.

Gracious Father, every arrow of financial loss that was fired into my life which resulted in my financial struggles, today that arrow is fired back to the sender and my financial status restored in the name of Jesus.

Heavenly Father, every devourer of resources which the enemy released into my life so that my finances are consumed on things that are completely unnecessary such as ill-health, I stand before the courts of heaven right now, and I pray that let that devourer be consumed by your fire and let the restoration of my finances happen now in the name of Jesus.

Holy Father, whatever divine idea that I have lost which has been generating my financial blessings, today I pray for the restoration of that divine idea in the name of Jesus.

Glorious Father, I have seen from your word that you can restore things and even human bodies. If you can restore these things to the perfect place that they were before an attack or loss, then restoring me to my past financial glory is not a difficult thing for you to do. Today I make demands for my financial restoration before the courts of heaven in the name of Jesus.

Righteous Father, any man or woman who is responsible for this financial loss upon my life and destiny, I pray before the courts of heaven right now that may your judgement come upon them in the name of Jesus.

Holy Father, I have seen from the life of Job that when the enemy made a loss to happen upon his life such that everything he had was gone, you restored to him double of what he previously had. Father, I pray in the courts of heaven that as a result of this financial restoration which you are making upon my life, it shall be a double portion for me in the name of Jesus.

Holy Father, any limitation that the enemy has placed upon my financial status such that whenever I get to a particular place in my financial life, a loss must occur. Today I stand before the courts of heaven, and I break that financial limitation and I make demands that the restoration of my finances happen now in the name of Jesus.

Holy Father, every projection from the pit of hell that is targeted at my finances, I stand before the courts of heaven today and I declare that projection from the pit of hell invalid in the name of Jesus.

Glorious Father, I come before your courts at this hour and I make demands that may the power of your presence cause a divine speed to happen in my life for my financial restoration in the name of Jesus.

Holy Father, I make demands before your courts at this hour for the impartation of the spirit of wisdom so that whenever you entrust financial resources into my hands again due to this restoration in the Courts of Heaven, I will not be wasteful with that financial resources again in the name of Jesus.

Righteous Father, if there is anything that is standing against my financial prosperity, I make demands for the removal of that thing before the courts of heaven in the name of Jesus.

Thank you, Holy Father, for hearing and answering all of my prayers because I know that from now henceforth a full financial restoration has been done in my life in the name of Jesus.

The favour

One of the greatest tools that the believer needs for the fulfilment of his life assignment on the earth is favour. Some doors can never open by prayer but by favour. There are things that you might have prayed about, answers are not apparent, but the moment you see favour either from the Lord or from man, the whole story can change in a single moment. It is for this reason that the enemy attacks the favour that a believer is supposed to enjoy because he knows that a believer that is living without the favour either of God or man, will struggle to complete the work that God has given him. What favour did you lose? Divine opportunities? Knocking once and doors open? Doors of financial favour? Whatever type of favour that you have been enjoying which was lost can be restored in the courts of heaven through courts of heaven prayer. The courts of heaven is a place for restoration and the God that you will meet in the courts of heaven is a God of restoration. If the favour that was in your life is lost, God can restore it in the Courts of Heaven. That is the type of God that we serve, the one that can restore all the things that you have lost in your life. As you go into the courts of heaven to pray for the restoration of the favour that was very active some time ago, God will restore it in the name of Jesus.

Reflection

Psalms 5:12

> *For thou, Lord, wilt bless the righteous;*
> *with favour wilt thou compass him as with*
> *a shield.*

Luke 2:52

And Jesus increased in wisdom and stature,
and in favour with God and man.

Prayer

Holy Father, I want to thank you for the opportunity and privilege that you have given to me to come before your courts at this moment and plead my case for the restoration of divine favour that I was enjoying. To you be all the glory and the honour, in the name of Jesus.

Gracious Father, I come before the courts of heaven to make my petition at this hour for my life and destiny, let the favour that I have been enjoying before the attack of the enemy upon my life be restored in the name of Jesus.

Holy Father, every arrow of disfavour that has been fired into my life and destiny which has made me continue to suffer disfavour, I come before the courts of heaven and I pray today that let that arrow of disfavour be returned to the sender and, the favour that I have missed be restored in the name of Jesus.

Gracious Father, You have said in your word in the book of Luke 2:52 that the boy Jesus grew in wisdom and favour both with man and God. I pray before the courts of heaven right now that let that same favour be activated over my life and destiny in the name of Jesus.

Holy Father, every garment of disfavour that the enemy has clothed me with, I stand before the courts of heaven, and I pray that let the fire that burns in the throne room of grace consume that garment of disfavour upon my life so that my favour is restored to me in full measure in the name of Jesus.

Righteous Father, everyone that is responsible for this attack of disfavour upon my life I pray today that let the fire that burns in the Courts of Heaven be released as a judgement upon them right now in the name of Jesus.

Holy Father, You have said in your word in the book of Psalms 5:12, that you are a God that surrounds your people with favour like a shield, I pray today by the power and authority in the name of Jesus that you will surround me with supernatural favour so that my life can be restored to the kind of favour I used to enjoy in the name of Jesus.

Heavenly Father, every projection of disfavour from the pit of hell that has made me miss a lot of opportunities in life today I stand before the courts of heaven, I pray that the projection of disfavour is cancelled by the blood of Jesus and my missed opportunities in life are restored in the name of Jesus.

Holy Father, I come before the courts of heaven to make my petition against the spirit of rejection which has been evident upon my life and destiny such that everywhere I go to, I get rejected for no reason. I make demands that let that garment of rejection that has been upon my life be burnt by fire, and you make restoration of my favour in the name of Jesus.

Righteous Father, in every area of my life that the enemy is trying to make a statement of disfavour today I stand before the courts of heaven, and I pray that the statement of disfavour over my life and destiny is cancelled in the name of Jesus.

Holy Father, I come before the courts of heaven at this time, and I pray that in every area of my life that I have missed favour (either in my business, career, destiny or even in my interaction with people that are supposed to help me fulfil my mission on earth) I pray in the Courts of Heaven today for the restoration of that missed favour in the name of Jesus.

Glorious Father, every financial favour that I have lost over the years in my life and destiny, today I stand before the courts of heaven to make this petition that the financial favour is restored by the power of your presence in the name of Jesus.

Righteous Father, every door of favour that the enemy has closed against my life and destiny which has caused me to begin to struggle right now, I pray in the courts of heaven that the door of favour is opened and restored in the name of Jesus.

Holy Father, if the disfavour that has come upon my life is as a result of my mistake, today I come before the courts of heaven, and I pray that your mercy which overflows from the throne of grace will be poured upon my life so that my favour is restored in the name of Jesus.

Thank you, Lord, for hearing and answering my prayers because I know from now henceforth that my favour has been fully restored to me in the name of Jesus.

Prayers for the Restoration of Doors of Life

Every human being that you see on the face of the earth created by God who has come to know and align with his maker, has been ordained by God to past through certain doors for the fulfilment of his life and destiny assignment. Once that man begins to pass through the doors that God has ordained for his life and destiny, that is where you will begin to see the supernatural in the life of that person, anything that the person touches with his hands is blessed beyond measure. And the devil is fully aware of this that is why he will close certain doors against some believers so that their life and destiny can be grounded. Whenever you have passed through a major door in your life and destiny, you will know it because things will begin to change suddenly. When I speak of doors, I'm not referring to businesses or finances alone. Even if you are a minister of the gospel, God has ordained for you to pass through certain doors before you can get to the place that he wants you to get to. If those doors that God has placed for you to pass through are closed, you can go nowhere. Some of you might have been soaring higher in ministry before. Others may have been experiencing great financial blessings before. For some people, there was a time that everything they touched exploded. This was as a result of a door that they have passed through. If a man has passed through the door of financial explosion, he will begin to experience uncommon financial multiplication in every area of his life. Is this biblical? Of course, it is. If what I am teaching you isn't biblical, I wouldn't have the right to say it. Paul the apostle was speaking in the book of 1 Corinthians 16:9 said that a door of effectual has been opened to me but there are many adversaries. For Paul the apostle, it was a ministry door that was opened to him. Although there is a lot of contention over the door that was opened to Paul the apostle. We will deal with that later because if we start teaching about doors and contention at the moment, we will digress from this teaching and prayer.

As a result of the door that was opened to Paul the apostle, his passage through that door, he was able to minister effectively to the people that the Lord has sent him to. For you, it may not be a ministry door. It may be a business door, financial door, favour door, divine connection doors, et cetera. These are the reasons why the enemy tries to shut doors against the lives of believers on the earth. The devil knows that once he has been able to succeed against the life of a believer by shutting the door against his life, that believer cannot go anywhere. And how do you know that a door has been closed against you? You know that a door has been closed against you whenever you discover that the things that you have been enjoying have stopped completely. For instance, if it is a financial door that was closed against your life and destiny, you will certainly discover that the channel through which the finances were flowing suddenly closed with no reason or explanation. And every attempt at doing the same thing you were doing that is bringing financial resources into your hands, yielded no result. If you have been experiencing anything like that then a financial door has been closed against your life. I mainly used the example of finances, it could be in other areas of your life.

Friends, I want you to understand that you are dealing with God who can restore to you all doors that have been closed against your life and destiny. If it is a door that you are enjoying that was suddenly closed either because of your mistake or even the attack of the enemy, the God of restoration in the courts of heaven will restore that door to the status it used to be before. And that is what we shall be praying in a couple of moments for the restoration of doors that have been closed against your life and destiny.

Reflection

1 Corinthians 16:9

> *For a great door and effectual is opened unto me, and there are many adversaries.*

2 Corinthians 2:12

> *Furthermore, when I came to Troas to preach Christ's gospel, and a door was opened unto me of the Lord,*

Prayer

Holy Father, I come before your throne of grace to appreciate you for the wonderful opportunity and privilege that you have given to me to come before the courts of heaven to pray for the restoration of doors that were suddenly closed against my life. To you be all the glory and the honour in the name of Jesus.

Heavenly Father, I come before you today, and I ask for the restoration of all doors that have been closed against my life and destiny in the name of Jesus.

Righteous Father, every human being that is supposed to serve as a door for me to pass to where I am supposed to go to as ordained by you, and that door has been closed against my life and destiny, I pray for the restoration of that door in the name of Jesus.

Gracious Father, where the doors of favour have been shut down against my life and destiny, I pray for the restoration of those doors in the name of Jesus.

Holy Father, every witchcraft activity that is responsible for the shutting down of doors of my life, I pray today that before the courts of heaven that you will release your fire to consume those witchcraft activities and all their practitioners, and that those doors that witchcraft attacks have shut against my life be restored in the name of Jesus.

Gracious Father, where I have shut down the doors of my life as a result of personal mistakes, I stand before the courts of heaven today, and I make my petition for your mercy. You have said in your word that your mercy is greater than your judgement therefore I pray today that your mercy will reach out to me and cause all of the doors that I have shut as a result of my mistake in life to be restored in the name of Jesus.

Holy Father, I come before you today to make my petition in the Courts of Heaven that you will cause a restoration of every ministry door that has been closed against my life and destiny in the name of Jesus.

Holy Father, I come before the courts of heaven to pray for the restoration of the doors of divine favour and opportunities closed against my life and destiny, I make demands that those doors are restored in the name of Jesus.

Righteous Father, every door of divine wisdom that has been shut against my life by the enemy, today I pray for the restoration of that door in the name of Jesus.

Glorious Father, anything that has been serving as a hindrance to the doors I am supposed to enter in life, I pray that let those hindrances be removed in the name of Jesus.

Heavenly Father, I pray for the release of supernatural wisdom on how to open doors of my life and destiny before the courts of heaven right now in the name of Jesus.

Gracious Father, every attempt of the enemy to shut any other door in the future against my life and destiny, I stand before the courts of heaven, and I pray that the plan of the enemy is cancelled in the name of Jesus.

Thank you, Father, for hearing and answering my prayers before the courts of heaven for the restoration of doors shut against my life and destiny. To you be all the glory and the honour in the name of Jesus.

Business Restoration

The Bible tells us that the path of the just is as a shining light that will continue to shine unto the perfect day. If the Lord wants to bless a man one of the ways he does that is through the release of business ideas in the life of that person. It doesn't matter what type of business provided that business is meant for the believer, he will prosper in it. And do you know even God is a businessman by the way he acts? He gave the life of his Son Jesus Christ so that he will be able to harvest more souls. In essence, he planted Jesus as the seed so that he will be able to get many other seeds through the life of his Son, Jesus Christ. In the book of:

Luke 19:12-20

12 He said therefore, A certain nobleman went into a far country to receive for himself a kingdom, and to return.

13 And he called his ten servants, and delivered them ten pounds, and said unto them, Occupy till I come.

14 But his citizens hated him, and sent a message after him, saying, We will not have this man to reign over us.

15 And it came to pass, that when he was returned, having received the kingdom, then he commanded these servants to be called unto him, to whom he had given the money, that he might know how much every man had gained by trading.

16 Then came the first, saying, Lord, thy pound hath gained ten pounds.

17 And he said unto him, Well, thou good servant: because thou hast been faithful in a very little, have thou authority over ten cities.

18 And the second came, saying, Lord, thy pound hath gained five pounds.

19 And he said likewise to him, Be thou also over five cities.

20 And another came, saying, Lord, behold, here is thy pound, which I have kept laid up in a napkin:

We saw how God gave money to his servants to invest to multiply it, and when he came back, he demanded from the servants how they have used the money that he has given them. The one that was given ten silver, went and multiplied and it became twenty. The one that was given five pieces of silver, multiplied it and it became ten. And the other who was given one piece of silver went and planted it in the ground, and it never multiplied. When the master came back to demand from the servant the inventory of how they have used the resources he had entrusted into their hands, the servant that has one was severely condemned into eternal darkness because he did not know how to multiply it.

Friends, God is also a businessman is just that the way he does business is different, and we will look at it. Why do you think that God released the Holy Spirit into your life? Why has the Lord surrounded your life with angels? Why did God put a protective hedge over your life? Do you think all of this divine investment is a waste? God is protecting his investment. There is something in your life that God has been steadily investing into, and he is hoping that one day, he will profit from your life through the kind of lifestyle that you will lead which in the long run will bring glory to his name. All the divine investment that God has been making in your life can be regarded as a business. He's investing in you today as a child of God so that your life can become profitable for winning souls for him tomorrow. Is that not a business?

So business did not start from you it was invented by God who has been doing it even before we were created. He invested his life into us so that we can be profitable to him for the service of mankind. He invested himself into Lucifer so that he can offer to him worship although he later fell. So every business that God has entrusted into your hands is for multiplication so that it can be a source of finance to you and a blessing to those around your life.

Since the devil knows that whatever God has entrusted into the hands of a believer will multiply because the Bible says whatsoever that is born of God overcomes the world, he attacks the businesses of believers all the time.

The only condition is that the business should not be your invention, but it should be something that God has shown you or led you to. Once it is the Lord that has led you into the business, it must overcome, that is multiplication. The only problem is many a believer is doing what he prefers rather than depending on the Holy Spirit to show him what he is supposed to do as a business.

So when you see the devil laying siege against your business it is because he is afraid of the multiplication that is to follow thereafter. The devil knows that the resources in the hands of a believer is a tool of warfare. One believer can decide to sponsor a Gospel Crusade that will lead to the harvest of souls. In the Ministry of Reinhard Bonnke, many believers were sponsoring the messages he was preaching all over the world especially in Africa where his ministry is primarily based. And can I shock you? Some of the people who sponsored these preaching of the gospel are businessmen and women around the world. Do you see why the devil has been attacking your business now? He knows that money in the hands of the believer who understand the principles of the covenant and the Holy Spirit, the principle of giving and receiving, is a destructive weapon of warfare against the kingdom of darkness. One believer can build a church. A single believer can engage in welfare packages for the less privileged and as a result of that, people may see the light of the kingdom of God and give their lives to Christ. So the attack of the devil against your business is not a mere attack, but one that is targeted towards the expansion of the kingdom of God. He knows that if you are living in financial struggles because of the attack upon your business, you can do little or no damage to him. He also knows that when you are financially empowered, the foundation of hell will be shaking because of the money in your hands.

Friends, I want you to understand that the attack of the enemy upon your life especially as regards your business goes beyond you. The enemy is attacking what your money will do for the expansion and growth of the kingdom of God. There are many believers today who will go to heaven and will receive greater rewards than many pastors as a result of their investment of financial resources into the work of the expansion of the kingdom of God. You might not have seen them preached the gospel anywhere but whenever they release financial resources which God has blessed through their business into the kingdom of God, God looks at it that they have also preached that gospel because without their finances the messages won't have been preached. Do you have a business and the enemy is attacking you? Is your business lost? Are you worried that you used to have a lot of financial overflow from your business but today that business has virtually disappeared? It doesn't matter what has happened, the God of restoration whom you will meet in the courts of heaven will make restoration of your business in the name of Jesus.

Reflection

Romans 8:28

> *And we know that all things work together for good to them that love God, to them who are the called according to his purpose.*

Philippians 1:6

> *Being confident of this very thing, that he which hath begun a good work in you will perform it until the day of Jesus Christ:*

Prayer

Holy Father, I want to thank you for the special opportunity that you have granted to me to come before your courts at this hour and to make a petition for the restoration of my business. I am not taking this opportunity of direct access to the courts of heaven for granted, and I am saying let your name be glorified and magnified in the name of Jesus.

Holy Father, I stand before the courts of heaven to make this petition in this manner, if this business that was lost was as a result of my mistake and negligence or the disobedience of instruction that you have given me, I stand before the courts of heaven at this hour, and I plead for your mercy in the name of Jesus.

Heavenly Father, I stand before the courts of heaven today and I make demands for the restoration of my divine business ideas in the name of Jesus.

Righteous Father, every profit that has been lost in my business I come before you today to make a petition in the Courts of Heaven because I know that you are a God of restoration and whoever that works with you, will have everything that he has lost restored. If you can restore coins, human bodies, and animals, then the restoration of my profit is but a light thing before you. I ask before your courts at this hour for a full restoration of my profit in the name of Jesus.

Holy Father, I have seen from your word that when the devil attacked the life of Job so that he lost everything he had, the God of restoration restored to him everything in double fold. I pray that you will restore to me double of what I have lost in the name of Jesus.

Holy Father, let the power that is available in your presence cause a restoration to happen in my business right now in the name of Jesus.

Heavenly Father, there is no attack on my business that the devil has brought that is too great for you to handle. By the power of your presence today in the courts of heaven I pray for the destruction of every attack of the enemy upon my business and let the destruction of that attack of the enemy lead to the restoration of my business in the name of Jesus.

Holy Father, every limitation that the enemy has placed upon my business today that limitation is broken in the name of Jesus.

Holy Father, I make demands right now in the Courts of Heaven that whatever it is that the enemy has been using against the rise of my business, let it be destroyed in the name of Jesus.

Glorious Father, I know that you are a God of restoration because you have said in your word that you will restore to me all the years that the caterpillar and the cankerworms have eaten from me, I pray for the restoration of all the years that the enemy has eaten of my business in the name of Jesus.

Holy Father, by the fire that burns in the throne room of grace, let the fire be released upon every witchcraft attack over my business so that a complete restoration can take immediate effect in the name of Jesus.

Gracious Father, you have said in your word that no weapon formed against me shall prosper. In the same vein, no weapon that is formed against my business shall prosper. Every attack on my business in the future which the enemy has planned to execute, by the power in the name of Jesus that attack is destroyed in the name of Jesus.

Holy Father, I stand before your throne of grace right now, and I make demands for the release of the divine wisdom idea that I need for my business to get to its next level in the name of Jesus.

Gracious Father, I know that you are a God that can make a restoration. And I know that there is no restoration that you can't make no matter how bad the attacks of the enemy might be. I have come into the courts of heaven where the concentrated power of your presence is felt. I pray that as you restore my business, a divine speed will be released into my business for supernatural growth in the name of Jesus.

Holy Father, in any area of my life that the enemy is laying claim to my business, I stand before the courts of heaven, and I break that legal ground in the name of Jesus.

Gracious Father, you have said in your word that by the anointing shall every yoke be broken. I make demands upon the anointing of the One that seats upon the throne of grace and administers all the activities of both eternity and mortality in the Courts of Heaven, let that anointing break every yoke of darkness over my business in the name of Jesus.

Thank you, Lord, for the restoration of my business and the divine speed that has been attached to that restoration. I know that my business will begin to move from one level of glory to another through the power of the prayer of restoration I have made in the Courts of Heaven today. Thank you, Lord, in Jesus name.

Prayers for Restoration of Marriage relationship/relationships

This prayer is for those who have lost their marriage or relationship that God has ordained for them, and they are trusting God for the restoration of that relationship. If you are in a relationship that is supposed to lead to marriage or the marriage had been broken either as a result of your mistake or even an attack of the enemy, I want to let you know that God is a God of restoration and in the courts of heaven, God can restore your marriage or relationship. When God is bringing two people together either for marriage or a relationship, he has a reason for doing that. So whenever you notice the attack of the enemy upon either your marriage or your relationship that is supposed to lead to marriage, the devil isn't attacking you. He is attacking the purpose of that relationship because he knows that the coming together of two believers under God either for marriage or relationship means trouble for his kingdom. So the enemy will do everything in his capacity to ensure that either the relationship gets destroyed before it leads to marriage or the marriage is broken during its lifetime.

Friends, I want to let you know that your marriage can be restored. I also want to let you know that your relationship can be restored. Although some of us may be opened to the idea of a divorce, the Bible makes us understand that in the book of Malachi God hates divorce. He didn't bring it together so that your marriage will end just like that. Neither did the Lord lead you into that relationship so that it will crash. Most of these are attacks of the enemy but the believer may not understand that the enemy is attacking that relationship or marriage. They may say, my husband is the problem. He may say, my wife, is the problem. It is also possible to hear believers complaining, that my fiancé is the problem. However, if we look critically into the root cause of the problem we will discover that it is an attack of the enemy so that the marriage is either prevented from taking place or the marriage relationship is destroyed. If that is your case, you have come to the God of restoration and in the courts of heaven, a speedy restoration of either your relationship or marriage will take place in the name of Jesus.

Reflection

Matthew 19:6

Wherefore they are no more twain, but one flesh. What therefore God hath joined together, let not man put asunder.

Ecclesiastes 4:9

Two are better than one; because they have a good reward for their labour.

Prayer

Holy Father, I bless your name for the wonderful opportunity and privilege of direct access to the Courts of Heaven for prayers for the restoration of my relationship or marriage to you be all the glory in the name of Jesus.

Heavenly Father, in any area of my life that I have made a mistake which has cost me my relationship or marriage, I come before the courts of heaven at this moment, and I am asking you to show me your mercy and forgiveness in the name of Jesus.

Holy Father, I know from your word that you are a God of restoration, and there is nothing that is too damaged to be restored. No relationship is too damaged to be restored. No marriage is too scattered to be restored. I stand before your courts to make demands at this moment that restoration is effected upon my marriage/relationship in the name of Jesus.

Glorious Father, every attack of the enemy which has led to the loss of my marriage/relationship, I come before the courts of heaven because I know that you are a God of restoration with great ability to restore anything no matter how lost it may be. I pray today that my marriage/relationship will be restored in the name of Jesus.

Holy Father, every arrow of attack that the enemy has fired into my life which has led to the loss of my marriage/relationship, I make demands today for a complete restoration in the name of Jesus.

Glorious Father, I have seen from your word that the prophet Jeremiah was in the wilderness and you make him pray for the restoration of the dead. I make demands at this hour before the courts of heaven that no matter how dead my relationship/marriage may be, let the restoration power that is available in the courts of heaven caused the restoration of that marriage/relationship in the name of Jesus.

Holy Father, as you cause this restoration in my relationship/marital life, I pray that the wine of that relationship be restored too in the name of Jesus.

Gracious Father, as a result of this restoration which you have done in the courts of heaven for my marital life/relationship, let the same purpose for which you have brought us together in the first instance be restored too in the name of Jesus.

Thank you, Lord, for hearing and answering all of my prayers to you be all the glory and the honour in the name of Jesus.

CHAPTER 6

Prayer Session B

In the previous chapter, we prayed for the restoration of physical things I believe that the Lord has made a restoration in the courts of heaven which will manifest in the realm of the physical. In this session of prayer, we shall be praying for the restoration of spiritual things. When I am talking about spiritual things, I am referring to what you have lost which is more spiritual than it is physical. It may not be visible to human eyes, the impact of that loss can be felt even in your life on the earth. The loss of spiritual things could be the loss of grace, divine wisdom, the loss of the voice of God, fervency in the spirit, fellowship, prayer altar, gifts and talents that have stopped manifesting. These are things that we can pray for their restoration in the courts of heaven. Some people have been enjoying a certain spiritual gift and all of a sudden it became lost. That loss could be as a result of either the inability to develop the gift or it is as a result of their interaction with certain evil practices which has damaged the gift. Now I need to create a balance because some of us may be thinking of the Scripture, the gifts and calling of God are without repentance. What the Scripture is referring to is that whenever God gives you a gift or talent or whatever you call it, he does not take it back. God has a lot of spiritual resources in his possession that the one he has given you is not even up to a tiny fragment of all that he has. So why would he collect it back? He gave the gift of worship to Lucifer, he never collects it back. However, the gift of Lucifer was damaged as a result of his rebellion. The Bible says that thou hast corrupted thy wisdom. So a gift may be damaged or a gift can be lost. Which is the reason why you will see some people who are experiencing the gift of revelation and dreams, and all of a sudden it stopped. It could be that it is damaged or it is lost. This is what we will be looking at in this session of prayer for the restoration of spiritual things that you have lost in the Courts of Heaven. And I believe that as you pray in the courts of heaven for the restoration of spiritual things which were lost, the God of restoration whom you are going to meet in the courts of heaven will cause out of his abundant mercy a restoration of your spiritual resources in the name of Jesus.

Prayers for the Restoration of Grace

Grace is the divine enablement that God has given to man to do what the strength of man can't do. Now, you have been reading my books and you have thoroughly enjoyed what I have been writing for a couple of years now. But can I tell you something about my writing, it is the grace of God. It is the grace for writing that the Lord has poured upon my life and destiny that has brought me to where I am today. Some people may desire to write and teach the word of the Lord through the power of their pen, but to them, the grace for writing may not have been released yet. I just discovered something during my high school that the desire to write was very strong in my life, yet I couldn't give expression to the gift that the Lord has poured on me until when the grace of God came upon my life. Do you see Benny Hinn today, there is a grace for ministry that the Lord has given him that empowers him to minister about the Holy Spirit in ways that others can't. Even Kenneth Hagin when he was alive, the grace of God was so strong upon his life that he taught faith above many of the ministers of his time. The factor of grace can be available in many facets of life. There is a grace for business and if you are a student in school, there is the grace for academic excellence that the Lord can pour into your life which will make you be above your contemporaries.

In the same way that this grace is available to you, that is how grace can be lost too. Whenever grace in any area of your life has been lost, you will notice what you use to do so freely and easily has turned to struggle. If you are in ministry and the grace of ministry has been lost, you will notice that the flawless way that you were moving in the ministry has suddenly changed and now you have begun to struggle.

My friends, when grace changes guard with struggle, such that what you have been doing without stress has now become a big challenge to you, pause and pray for restoration. And as we pray for the restoration of grace in the courts of heaven, the Lord will bring it back to you in the name of Jesus.

Paul the Apostle even reminded us that he is what he is by the grace of God. So in every area of your life that you desire to operate, there is the grace of God there that will help you become what you perfectly want to be. When that grace is lost, then you won't be able to work in that area effectively.

Reflection

2 Corinthians 9:8

> *And God is able to make all grace abound toward you; that ye, always having all*

> *sufficiency in all things, may abound to every good work:*

John 1:16

> *And of his fulness have all we received, and grace for grace.*

Prayers

Holy Father, I want to thank you for the wonderful opportunity that you have granted to me to come before the courts of heaven at this hour to you be all the glory and the honour in the name of Jesus.

Holy Father, I come before the courts of heaven to make a petition before your throne at this hour, and I ask that where I have lost grace in my life due to my mistakes and carelessness, I make demands for your mercy in the courts of heaven at this hour in the name of Jesus.

Holy Father, in every area of my life that I have lost grace such that the life of struggle has become the normal order, I pray today before the courts of heaven that there shall be a full restoration of that grace in the name of Jesus.

Gracious Father, where the loss of grace that is upon my life was as a result of pride because you have said in your word that you humble the proud and the humble one, you give him the grace. I ask today that you will show me mercy so that the root of that pride can be removed from my life in the name of Jesus.

Holy Father, that same grace that I have been enjoying before which has made me move at my speed, I make demands for the restoration of that same grace before the courts of heaven in the name of Jesus.

Holy Father, I want to be where you want me to by the power of your grace, and I pray that Lord God Almighty you will restore to me all the graces that I have lost in my life in the name of Jesus.

Heavenly Father, I make demands today before the courts of heaven for the restoration of that grace that you have given me to exist in the realm where you have ordained for me in the name of Jesus.

Gracious Father, I pray for the release of supernatural speed so that I can recover all that I have missed because of the loss of that grace in the name of Jesus.

Holy Father, I pray today that may your hand of grace from the courts of heaven come upon my life right now so that the restoration can take place for me to continue to do that which you have ordained me to do in life and for my destiny in the name of Jesus.

Holy Father, as you have made restoration of the grace that I have lost in my life, I pray for the ability to use it to your glory alone and not to make the same mistake that I have made in the past in the name of Jesus.

Thank you, Lord, because I am very certain that my prayers have been heard and answered. To you alone be all the glory as of the God of restoration in the courts of heaven in the name of Jesus.

Prayers for the Restoration of the Voice of God

Many believers may not understand this, but it is possible to lose the voice of God. In my few years of being a member of the body of Christ, I have seen countless stories of people who have lost the voice of God. One of the difficult areas for the devil to attack in the life of a man is hearing the voice of God. The worst he can do is to cause confusion so that you won't be able to discern the voice of God whenever he's speaking to you. But to stop God from talking to you, the devil doesn't have that type of power. And in many cases of the loss of the voice of God, is usually associated with either rebellion or carelessness on the part of the believer. Many times people confront me with this question, brother Pius, I used to hear his voice I don't know what happened again. I can no longer hear him. Whenever any believer comes to me with that kind of complaint, the first place I had to scrutinise is the level of obedience of that believer to the voice of God. You need to realise this fact, that God speaks to us by the Holy Spirit and the Bible has continuously warned us against grieving the Holy Spirit.

Whenever the Holy Spirit is talking to us, and we decided to disobey he is grieved by our disobedience. And I have stated this severally in some of my books about the Holy Spirit that he is one of the gentle personalities of the godhead. It is as a result of the gentility of the Holy Spirit that the father has provided for us in the Scripture not to grieve him. And who is at work on the earth at this moment? Of course, it is the Holy Spirit. In the time of Moses, it was the father that was operating on the earth. During the time of the apostles, it was Jesus that was operating on the earth. At this present dispensation, we have the third person of the Trinity, the Holy Spirit, who represent himself by the symbol of the dove, fire, wind, or even oil. I am not teaching you about the symbols of the Holy Spirit today as I do not want to digress from our main path. But disobedience is one of the chief culprits of the loss of the voice of God in the ears of the believer. When Saul started to disobey the voice of God that was coming through the Prophet Samuel, he lost all the ability to hear God through the three main channels he was hearing God – the dream, the prophet, and even by Urim.

1 Samuel 28:6

> *And when Saul inquired of the Lord, the Lord answered him not, neither by dreams nor by Urim, nor by prophets.*

If you have lost the voice of God in your life before, and you can go to the court of heaven and pray for mercy, the voice of God in your ears will be restored.

Friends, if the voice of God used to sound in your ear before and all of a sudden it was lost either because of disobedience or something you do not even understand, it is time to ask questions before you go to the courts of heaven prayers so that a restoration can take place. And I believe that as you go into the courts of heaven to pray for the restoration of the voice of God in your ears, the Lord will be merciful to you so that you can start hearing him again. Every child of God needs to hear the voice of God because it is one of the ways through which we can be led by the spirit of God.

Reflection

Isaiah 30:21

> *And thine ears shall hear a word behind thee, saying, This is the way, walk ye in it, when ye turn to the right hand, and when ye turn to the left.*

John 10:27

> *My sheep hear my voice, and I know them, and they follow me:*

Prayer

Holy Father, thank you for the access to your presence and the courts of heaven at this moment so that I can make my petition before the throne of grace to you be all the glory and the honour in the name of Jesus.

Holy Father, I come before your Courts of Heaven at this hour to plead my cause of mercy before you. And I ask that in any area of my life that I have been rebellious which has resulted in the loss of the voice of God, I pray today for mercy in the name of Jesus.

Glorious Father, in any area of my life that I have been rebellious to the voice of God which has resulted in the loss of the voice of God, I pray for forgiveness and your mercy so that it can lead to a restoration of the voice of God in my ears in the name of Jesus.

Holy Father, I know how important your voice is to the life of a believer and I make demands today in the courts of heaven for a complete restoration of your voice in my ears in the name of Jesus.

Holy Father, I know that delayed obedience is no obedience at all. And I am fully aware that delayed obedience can lead to the loss of the voice of God. Today I make an application for the grace not to delay in obeying you in the name of Jesus.

Heavenly Father, I make demands today before your Courts for the release of the supernatural grace of obedience to the Holy Spirit in my life in the name of Jesus.

Righteous Father, You have said in your word that we should not grieve the Holy Spirit. I know that it is through the Holy Spirit that you speak to me and whenever he is grieved, I can't hear the voice of God. I make demands today for the release of that grace so that I will not grieve the Holy Spirit in the name of Jesus.

Holy Father, where the spirit has been impressing anything on my heart to do that I have failed to obey promptly as it was impressed upon the tablets of my heart, I ask for mercy and forgiveness in the mighty name of Jesus.

Righteous Father, I have seen from your word that Saul was rebellious to your counsel an instruction and as a result of that he lost the voice of God. In any way at all that my disobedience has led to the loss of the voice of God, I pray for mercy and forgiveness today in the name of Jesus.

Holy Father, I come before your courts today to make a demand before you in the same way that the voice of God used to sound in my ears that is how I pray for the restoration of the voice of God in my life at this moment in the name of Jesus.

Gracious Father, anything at all that had taken the voice of God from my life and destiny, I pray today that you will restore it before the courts of heaven in the name of Jesus.

I praise you, Lord because I know that you have heard and answered all of my prayers. I am fully persuaded that the voice of God has been restored into my life. And from today onward, I will begin to hear your voice again the way I used to in the name of Jesus.

Prayers for the Restoration of Gifts and Talent

Before I proceed into the teaching proper, I want to make something very clear to you. Although I have said it in another aspect of the prayer, and I will state it again. The gifts and calling of God are without repentance. Whenever the Lord has given you any gift, he does not take it back. However, a gift can be lost. Several people used to have dreams and revelation before, all of a sudden no more. That was the gift of dreams. There was a time in my life that I used to have the gift of interpretation of dreams so abundantly but it stopped. And any time I want to interpret any dream, I would struggle. So I went to the Lord and ask what happened, and he told me what I did wrong that led to the loss of the gift of interpretation of dreams. When I did that, the Lord restored my gift to me and I could interpret dreams like I used to do. Was it that the gift was taken away by

God, not at all. The gift was there. But it could not be operated as a result of something I did wrong.

Friends, I do not know what gift and talent that you have which had been lost. I want to let you know that the God of restoration in the courts of heaven is more than capable to restore it to you through the abundance of his mercies.

Reflection

1 Peter 4:10

> *As every man hath received the gift, even so minister the same one to another, as good stewards of the manifold grace of God.*

Proverbs 18:16

> *A man's gift maketh room for him, and bringeth him before great men.*

Prayer

Holy Father, I want to thank you for the access to the courts of heaven which you have given me right now to you be all the glory and honour in the name of Jesus.

Heavenly Father, whatever mistakes that I have made that caused the loss of my gift and talent, today I pray for your mercy to come over my life in the name of Jesus.

Glorious Father, I come before you to make a petition for the restoration of the sharpness of my gift and talent. That cutting edge ability that I used to have in my talent and gift has been lost. I pray right now before the courts of heaven that you will cause a restoration of that sharpness of my gift and talent in the name of Jesus.

Holy Father, as you have made the restoration of the sharpness of my gift and talent, I pray before the courts of heaven that I will use that gift and talent to the glory and the honour of your name and for kingdom expansion on the earth in the name of Jesus.

Gracious Father, I come before your courts at this hour to make demands for restoration to be done upon my life and destiny so that my gift and talent will work the way it used to in the name of Jesus.

Holy Father, I come before the courts of heaven and I make demands for complete restoration of all gifts, graces, ability, and talent that you have released upon my life and destiny in the name of Jesus.

Holy Father, in any area of my life that I employ the use of my gift either for personal aggrandizement or to serve the purpose of the world, I pray today for your mercy in the name of Jesus.

Heavenly Father, let the power of your presence in the courts of heaven touch my gift and talent so that it can be very effective after restoration in the name of Jesus.

Righteous Father, I pray today in the Courts of Heaven in the same way that my gifts and talent have been able to touch the lives of so many people, let the restoration that you have made bring the same ability of the gift to reach to many people in the kingdom of God and beyond in the name of Jesus.

Thank you, Holy Father, because I know that my prayers have been answered as this is the confidence I have in you whenever I come before the courts of heaven, I am fully persuaded that you have heard and answered me. Be glorified Lord, in the name of Jesus.

Prayer for the Restoration of Fellowship

Fellowship with God can be lost too. And it doesn't matter what resulted in the loss of fellowship. This is the reason why sometimes you find it very difficult to understand that you haven't prayed for a long time, yet your spirit isn't troubling you. The life that God has created man to live is a life of dependence upon him daily. A man was not created to exist independent of God. As you fellowship with God daily, you can draw strength from your walk with him. Several things can destroy your fellowship with God beyond sin. And whenever fellowship is lost, you need to take steps to have it restored. The strength of the believer is not far away from his fellowship life. The stronger the believer is in terms of his fellowship with God, the more radiant and powerful his life will be. So whenever you notice that you have been disconnected from the place of fellowship, you have to act very fast to be restored. You can go into the courts of heaven and pray for the restoration of your fellowship life, you can pray ordinary prayers for the restoration of your fellowship too. But by no means should you stay without taking a step towards the restoration of your fellowship with God.

The devil is very aware that the strength of a man is not in man himself. The strength of a man is in his fellowship with God. And once the devil can disconnect you from the place of fellowship, he has disconnected you from the place of your strength. The whole attack in the Garden of Eden was targeted towards one purpose, the destruction of the fellowship that man has been enjoying with God. And when the devil was able to successfully disconnect Adam and Eve from the life that God has ordained for them in the place of fellowship, the divine life that Adam and Eve had was gone until the coming of Jesus was able to restore man to God.

Friends, whenever you notice that prayer has become a very hard thing to do. The study of the Bible has become so difficult that you can go weeks without studying your Bible and nothing bothers you. Whenever you notice that your passion for the place of fellowship has died completely, and you no longer care whether you spend time with God or not, it is time to run into the place of prayer for the restoration of your fellowship with God.

In my life, I have experienced several times where my fellowship with God was disconnected. Prayer becomes a very difficult thing to do. The study of the word becomes very difficult to do. And everything seems to be like a struggle. That was a sign to me that I needed the restoration of my fellowship with God. And many of the times that I experience something like this, I lift my hands to the Lord for help, and he has always heard me.

We are going to be praying at this moment for the restoration of our fellowship. If you have been praying before, you notice that you can't pray now. If you have been studying the word of God effectively, and you notice that everything is gone. If you have lost contact with the place of prayer and fellowship, this prayer is for you. I want you to know that God can restore that which you have lost including spiritual things such as fellowship.

Reflection

2 Corinthians 13:14

> *The grace of the Lord Jesus Christ, and the love of God, and the communion of the Holy Ghost, be with you all. Amen.*

1 Thessalonians 5:17

Pray without ceasing

Prayer

Holy Father, thank you for the special privilege that you have given me to come before the courts of heaven at this time to pray for the restoration of my fellowship with you. I am not taking this privilege for granted to you be all the glory and the honour for this access to the courts of heaven at this time in the name of Jesus.

Heavenly Father, I stand before your courts at this time to make demands for the restoration of my fellowship with you. I pray for the complete restoration of my fellowship with you in the name of Jesus.

Holy Father, anything that the devil has taken from my prayer life which has made me become very prayerless, I come before your throne at this time, and I pray for restoration in the name of Jesus.

Glorious Father, I pray today before the courts of heaven that after this restoration of my prayer life, it will enjoy a leap from this present level to the next level in the name of Jesus.

Holy Father, every limitation that the enemy has placed upon my fellowship life through the attack of the devil, that limitation is removed and destroyed in the name of Jesus.

Heavenly Father, I ask for the release of your fire from your presence in the courts of heaven to come upon my prayer life and my fellowship with you right now in the name of Jesus.

Righteous Father, I make demands right now before the courts of heaven that you will baptise me with your fire and passion for the place of fellowship and prayer in the name of Jesus.

Gracious Father, let the fire that comes out from your presence land upon my prayer altar right now in the name of Jesus.

Holy Father, You have said in your word that you will restore to me all the years that the caterpillar and the cankerworms have eaten from me. I pray today before the courts of heaven, and I ask that everything that the enemy has made me miss as a result of my disconnection from fellowship with you, I pray that let there be a complete restoration of those things that I have missed in the name of Jesus.

Gracious Father, I make demands at this hour before your courts, and I pray that whatever it is that makes people dwell in your presence in fellowship without getting tired, I pray that you will pour that grace upon my life at this moment in the name of Jesus.

Holy Father, where I have demonstrated weakness in the place of fellowship today I pray that you will touch my life like never before with your fire for fellowship in the name of Jesus.

Heavenly Father, I make demands for the release of the grace of fellowship upon my life at this moment in the name of Jesus.

Thank you, Lord, for hearing and answering my prayer at this hour to you be all the glory and the honour because I know that from now forward a complete restoration of my fellowship life with you has been done according to your mercies in the name of Jesus.

Prayer for the Restoration of Fervency

Fervency in the spirit is the fire that should sustain the life of every believer while serving the Lord. When I talk about having fervency, I'm referring to the passion with which you serve God and the fire that the service is effected. The attack of the enemy upon the life of a believer can be diverse, one of the greatest targets of the enemy is the fervency of that child of God. The devil is aware that if we are serving God with fervency, the blessings of God will rest upon our lives. In the book of Exodus 23:25-26, the Bible clearly explains to us the benefit of service. The Bible says serve the Lord your God and he will bless your bread and water. He will take sickness from the midst of you and the number of your days God has promised that he will fulfil it. So whenever the devil is attacking your fervency, he is not only attacking your service but the entirety of your Christian life.

So when your fervency is under the siege of the enemy, and you notice that you begin to serve God as if you are being forced, then there is a problem. In this case, you may need to go into the courts of heaven for the restoration of your fervency. Some so many believers have lost their fervency. And how do you know that you have lost your fervency? Whenever you notice that the things you used to do before, you have stopped doing them with the same passion then you have lost your fervency. I will give you some examples to drive home this teaching. When you gave your life to Christ, what was one of the commonest desires that you have? Many had the desire to win souls for Christ, and they never stop sharing the gospel that got them saved. Others had a burning desire and passion to do one thing or the other for the Lord. Yet for some whenever you look for them they are always in the place of fellowship with the Lord and the zeal for the Lord is undying. But is it the same today? That is the fundamental question to answer so that you can know whether you are still fervent for the Lord or not. When you begin to see that the level of your fervency for the Lord has dropped, then you need to pray for the restoration of your fervency so that you can serve the Lord as the Bible has commanded us, fervent in spirit serving the Lord.

I pray that as you go to the courts of heaven for the restoration of our fervency, God will bring back the same passion and fire we used to have for him back in those days in the name of Jesus.

Reflection

Romans 12:11

> *Not slothful in business; fervent in spirit; serving the Lord*

Ephesians 6:18

> *Praying always with all prayer and supplication in the Spirit, and watching thereunto with all perseverance and supplication for all saints;*

Prayer

Holy Father, I thank you for the direct access to the courts of heaven to pray for the restoration of my fervency be magnified and glorified in the name of Jesus.

Heavenly Father, I come before the courts of heaven to pray for the restoration of my fervency in the spirit. I pray today that you will restore my passion and fire for you in totality in the name of Jesus.

Glorious Father, in the same way, that you can baptise people with your fire according to your word which says that thereafter comes he whose shoe latches I am not worthy to lose. He is the one that will baptise you with fire. I pray for the baptism of fire and passion for you in the name of Jesus.

Holy Father, in the same way, that you baptise people with the Holy Spirit so they can live the life of fire and passion for you, I pray for a fresh baptism of the Holy Spirit for the restoration of my fervency in the spirit in the name of Jesus.

Holy Father, every spirit of lethargy that has crept into my life which has destroyed my fervency, today I pray for the fresh release of the breath of God from the courts of heaven so that the lethargy is destroyed out of my life and destiny in the name of Jesus.

Holy Father, I make demands before the courts of heaven at this time that you will cause a release from your throne of the grace for fervency upon my life and destiny right now in the name of Jesus.

Glorious Father, I know that this is an attack upon my fervency because the devil does not want me to take full benefit of service. I come before the courts of heaven at this moment, and I pray for destruction of every attack of the enemy upon my life and destiny in the name of Jesus.

Holy Father, whatever it is that the enemy has placed upon my life and destiny to limit my fervency, that limitation is removed in the Courts of Heaven at this moment in the name of Jesus.

Thank you, Holy Father, for the restoration of my fervency in the courts of heaven to you be all the glory and the honour in the mighty name of Jesus.

CHAPTER 7

Orders of Restoration

In a typical court system, whenever a case has come before the judge and trial proceeded until it was concluded at the end of that proceeding of the court, an order of that court would be given and all the parties concerned have no choice but to obey that order that the court gave. Irrespective of the feelings that the parties may have concerning the order of the judge, they are bound by it. It is not a matter of choice, it is a matter of command.

As it is in the typical earthly court system, so it is also in the courts of heaven. The Bible makes us understand that what we see on the earth is the shadow of the things to come. God sits on his throne in the courts of heaven to administer the whole of eternity and mortality and whatever he says, stands. It doesn't matter what the devil thinks about what God has said. It also doesn't matter what any mortal man or an angel thinks about what God has said, is a command that is coming from the courts of heaven where God administers the earth and eternity. In the book of Philippians 2: 5-11, the Bible says at the mention of the name of Jesus every knee must bow and every tongue must confess that Jesus is Lord. I want you to look critically at the above Scripture under reference that the instruction given in that passage is a must. So whenever the name of Jesus is mentioned, a command is issued to all demons, powers, principalities, situations, circumstances, things that you have lost to be restored. That is the power in the name of Jesus. It doesn't matter what a person or principality or even authority thinks about the order that God has given. At the beginning of creation when God was creating the earth, he was not doing a negotiation process where he said maybe light you can appear any time you want to. Or darkness if you desire to go, just go. But it was a command, let there be light and the Bible proceeded further, there was light.

Whenever God is sitting in the Courts of Heaven that is a kind of command or orders that he gives. Imagine that what you have been praying for restoration is in the hands of another person or even power or force, when you are praying in the Courts of Heaven and God gives an order concerning what belongs to you which was lost, they have no choice but obey by releasing it back to you. It is for this reason that there is no limitation to the things that God can restore to you. We have seen that

God can restore things, bodies, and anything that he desires to make a restoration. That is the power of the restoration that God can make in the courts of heaven ordering the things that belong to you to be given back to you. And in case what is missing is not in the hands of any man, God can make an order restoring it. Remember the asses of Saul's father that were missing that he went looking for, the Bible did not tell us that it was stolen. The Bible said that the asses were missing. Yet there was a restoration of that which was missing when Saul encountered the God of restoration through the life of the Prophet Samuel. The asses that were missing, were immediately found. That is what the God of restoration can do for you when he makes an order for restoration in your life. Whether they are things in the possession of other people or things that the enemy is holding or even things that are missing, an order of restoration by God works regardless. And as you go into the courts of heaven to pray for the restoration of what the enemy has stolen or in the hands of people or even the hands of powers and principalities, orders in the form of an answer to your prayer are going to be given in the name of Jesus.

Prayer for an Order of Restoration

Reflection

Proverbs 8:15

> *By me kings reign, and princes decree justice.*

1 Corinthians 4:20

> *For the kingdom of God is not in word, but in power.*

Prayer

Holy Father, I want to thank you for the access that you have given to me to come before the courts of heaven and to ask for orders of restoration to be made in my life to you be all the glory and the honour in the name of Jesus.

Righteous Father, whatever it is that belongs to me which is in the hands of another person, I pray before your courts at this hour and it is hereby ordered for that thing to be released into my hands in the name of Jesus.

Holy Father, by the order of the courts of heaven right now I pray for the restoration of everything that is missing in my life in the name of Jesus.

Holy Father, everything that belongs to me that is in the hand of any institution or authority by the order of the courts of heaven right now is restored in the name of Jesus.

Heavenly Father, whatever it is that belongs to me which has been taken, by the order of the courts of heaven is restored in the name of Jesus.

Righteous Father, I pray for an order before the courts of heaven restoring to me the financial glory that I was enjoying before the attack of the devil upon my finances in the name of Jesus.

Gracious Father, I pray for an order of the Courts of Heaven for the restoration of my health from the crown of my head down to the soles of my feet by the power in the name of Jesus.

Holy Father, I stand before the courts of heaven based on the Scripture that says anything that is missing in my life shall be restored and that God is a God of restoration who can restore to me all the years that the enemy has stolen from me. I ask before the courts of heaven for an order of restoration at this time restoring all that the enemy has taken from me in the name of Jesus.

Heavenly Father, I stand before the courts of heaven at this moment of prayer for the restoration of my family glory which by our mistakes and carelessness we allowed the devil to steal. I stand before the courts of heaven at this hour, and I pray for an order restoring all the glory that my family had in the name of Jesus.

Righteous Father, I pray before the courts of heaven at this hour that you will make an order for the complete restoration of my financial mantle in the name of Jesus.

Holy Father, I know that you are God of restoration and when I come before the courts of heaven to pray for restoration according to your will, you always hear me. Standing based on the Scripture that says ask and it shall be given to you, seek and you will find, knock and the door will be opened to you. I pray for an order of restoration of my place in ministry in the name of Jesus.

Glorious Father, I come before the courts of heaven at this hour to pray for an order of restoration so that what is in the hands of other people that belongs to me are released in the name of Jesus.

Heavenly Father, I ask for mercy whereby my attitude and character, I have chased away the destiny helpers that you have released into my life in the name of Jesus.

Holy Father, I know that you have shown me mercy and I have come before your throne and your courts at this hour to pray that you will make an order for the restoration of my destiny helpers in the name of Jesus.

Heavenly Father, I pray today before the courts of heaven and I asked that every door I am supposed to pass through for the fulfilment of my life assignment, be ordered opened before the courts of heaven in the name of Jesus.

Heavenly Father, I pray before the courts of heaven at this time for an order for the restoration of all graces that the enemy has stolen from my life and destiny in the name of Jesus.

Gracious Father, I stand before the courts of heaven for an order against all witchcraft attacks upon my life and destiny to cease at this moment in the name of Jesus.

Holy Father, I stand before the courts of heaven at this hour I pray before you Lord that every trap that the enemy has set for me either in the present or in the future, is ordered destroyed in the name of Jesus.

Thank you, Lord, for hearing and answering my prayers to you be all the glory and the honour in the name of Jesus.

Our Books

1.   Obtaining Restoration in the Courts of Heaven: Courtroom Prayers for All Round Restoration

2. Witchcraft Summons: Prayers for Overpowering witchcraft Summons & Refusing to Answer their Call

3. Monitoring Spirits: Prayers for Destroying Monitoring Spirits and Receiving Deliverance

4. Evil Gatekeepers: Prayers to Break Free, Enter and Possess what's Yours

5. Overthrowing Evil Altars Secrets Revealed: Prayers for Dismantling Evil Altars

6. Praying the Blood of Jesus the Right Way: Pleading the Blood of Jesus for Turnaround

7. Prayers that Destroy Water Spirits: Freedom from marine Kingdom and Marine Spirits

8. How to Cast out Demons: Expel Demons with Powerful Prayers of Victory

9. Courts of Heaven Prayers for your Children

10. Activating the Ministry of the Holy Spirit: Powerful Prayers to Unlock the Spirit Potentials

11. Operating in the Angelic Realm: Prayers that Activate the Ministry of Angels

12. Prayers that Delete Spiritual Marks: Powerful Prayers for Complete Deliverance from Spiritual Marks and Breakthroughs

23.   Prayers That Bring You Closer to the Holy Spirit: Powerful Prayers, Intense Reflection to Become the Closest Friend of the Holy Ghost (Holy Ghost Friendship Guide Book 3)

24.   Praying God's Promises to Reality: Simple Ways of Praying the Promises of God for Victory & Breakthrough

25.   God Wants You Protected From Disease

26.   Under His Divine Protection

27.   7 Day Fasting Challenge That Will Change Your Life Forever: 7 Powerful Prayers to Pray in 7 Days

28.   Praying Through the Book of Psalms for Financial Miracle: The Financial Miracle Prayer for Breakthrough

29.   Burning Evil Garments: Prayers That Destroy Evil Garments, Deliverance, Breakthroughs And God's Favour Into Your Life

30.   30 Days with the Holy Spirit: Powerful Prayers and Devotional for Personal Connection with the Holy Spirit and Be His Friend

31.   Breaking Evil Altars: Prayers, Decrees, Declarations for Dismantling Evil Altars

32.   How to see the Supernatural: Powerful Prayers that open the Unseen Realm